The Irish Influence
Migrant Workers in
Northern England

by Harold Slight

A Hayloft Publication

First published in 2000
by Hayloft Publishing,
Great Skerrygill, South Stainmore, Kirkby Stephen, Cumbria, CA17 4EU

Tel: 017683-42300 or Fax: 017683-41568
e-mail: icetalk@icetalk.co.uk
Web: www.hayloft.org.uk

ISBN 0 9523282 5 9

A catalogue record for this book is available from the British Library

Design, typesetting & production by Hayloft

Printed and bound by Lintons Printers, Durham

Front cover: Photograph by Peter Koronka

Contents

	Introduction	5
1.	The Canal Cutters	6
2.	The Canal Cutters - Carlisle to Port Carlisle	12
3.	The Coming of the Railways	14
4.	The Pipe Track Cutters	21
5.	The Tattie Howkers	24
6.	Tattie Howkers Bath Night	31
7.	The Flail Men	32
8.	The Paddy Lowpers	35
9.	The Irish Gypsies	37
10.	The Horse Dealers	46
11.	The Jack of all Trades	53
12.	The Irish Drovers	58
	Epilogue	60

O, for the days of the Kerry dancing
O, for the lilt of the piper's tune,
O, for one of those hours of gladness,
Gone alas, like our youth - too soon,

Some words from an old Irish song

Introduction

I have really enjoyed writing this account of a people who were my ancestors, - the farmers and drovers directly, the others indirectly, but all of them in the background somewhere.

My grandmother, Annie Cunningham, (father's mother) was descended from a long line of Irish story-tellers who kept the Irish past alive, when all writing was the prerogative of the wealthy. The story-teller was as much a part of the life of Ireland as the "horse whisperer" was to the equine world. The latter could calm even the most violent of beasts, by whispering a few sentences from some obscure language, in the ear of the horse. anyone who could capture the imagination of a small boy, and have that effect last for over seventy years, was capable of anything - she was!

When she told of driving over a hundred geese to the fair, while her brothers brought up the rear with a herd of cattle, you were there - you were part of the scene. When she told of tying corn sheaves after the brothers - you could nearly hear the swish of the scythe!

I have probably inherited my love of horses from those generations of horse-dealers, who brought their strings of horses across the Irish sea - of every breed, and for every purpose, and my interest in cattle, and sheep from the drovers who bought until they had a boat-load, then shipped these over the Irish sea to sell in the North of England.

When we settle down in our comfortable railway carriage seats, and are whisked away between those shiny rails to London, which we reach in a matter of two to three hours, when we talk glibly of progress, and the advanced state of the society in which we live, let us not forget that only a fraction of time separates us from the navvies camps and the sod shanties - from the slaving and often the dying, which made all this possible.

The Canal Cutters

D uring the eighteenth century, (the period of the start of the Industrial Revolution) it was decided that canals would be the cheapest form of transport for moving goods from one part of the country to another. whilst this provided work for a large number of our mainland nationalities boat-loads of Irish labourers were shipped in to to make the job quicker and cheaper. They brought with them their house-keepers, and camp-followers. The site of the workers' camps was the equivalent of today's African refugee camps. Most of them lived in sod shanties, either huts built of the thick grass sods cut from the line of the canal, plus the largest stones unearthed in the course of the work; or else the men cut a large room in the bank-side, big enough to hold six labourers and the "house-keeper", which was about the ratio. The door was thick sacking. All cooking was done in a big iron pot suspended on a chain over an open fire, - the whole weight supported by an iron tripod. Each man contributed his share to the pot, either by poaching, or buying cheap offal. The local butchers did a roaring trade at the navvy camps - even sheep's heads were in great demand.

By the time the canal was ready to fill with water, there was a shortage of game - both the furred, and feathered varieties - for five miles back on either side of the cut. Also, if the poachers came on a sheep caught by the horns in a thicket it too ended up in the pot.

The Irishmen started the day with bowls of watery oatmeal porridge cooked in the utilitarian iron pot. After the navvies had trudged away to their work the "house-keeper" began to bake the damper for their mid-day meal. This was a kind of unrisen bread, made from flour, water, and a pinch of salt, and baked on a flat iron skillet over the open fire, raising or lowering the chain, according to the amount of heat required. The damper was complemented by fried cheese, but it was cheese that you and I would have found inedible, frying it on the skillet which was greased with mutton-fat gave it a taste, and disguised its staleness. The grocers got rid of all their hard cheese in the navvies camp. About a quarter to twelve the house-keeper would head for the cut carrying six men's rations in two baskets.

The "cut" would be roughly a mile from the navigator camp, and she would join a band of women on the same errand. They would be a glad sight for their men, who would by this time be ravenously hungry. The meal was washed down by draughts of cold, weak, tea - if they could afford it. Milk and sugar were unknown commodities to the navigators.

The wise men saved a crust of damper, and a piece of fried cheese in their pockets for half past three, when the pang of hunger began to gnaw again. The house-keeper on the return journey would raid the nearest fields for turnips, or a potato patch, and the ill-gotten gains complemented the evening stew.

At this time very cottage kept a couple of pigs, curing one for the family, and selling one to finance the pair. In the curing process, when the quarters hung drying from the bacon hooks next to the kitchen range, a steel knitting needle was periodically thrust into them as far as the bone. If there was the slightest dampness, and a sweat on the point when it was withdrawn, it was deemed that the quarter had been invaded by the dreaded "bacon bee", (a form of maggot) and it had to be boiled, and eaten fairly quickly. If however they lived near the navvies camp, it was not such a tragedy. It could be sold to the Irishmen and made a welcome change to their diet for at least a week.

The construction companies relied as much on the strength of a human frame, as those who built the Pharaoh's Pyramids. three men of the six were engaged in cutting, and throwing back the soil and stones - their tools were mattocks, spades, and shovels and crowbars for awkward boulders.

Two of the men had a wheelbarrow each, and were responsible for clearing their section of the cut. The tools they used were shovels and spades. The sixth member of the half dozen, although usually a lad or an old man who could not have stood much heavy work, was perhaps the key member of the team - he was in charge of the horse! To call it a horse was a euphemism. It was usually too old for heavy farm work, or lame or a combination of both - either ensured that it

was cheap!

As long as the animal could pull a barrow load of spoil up the cut-bank, that was all the Irishmen required. The method used was this - a post was driven in to the top of the cut-bank, to which an iron pulley was fixed. The horse was brought to the post and reversed; then a rope attached to the swingletree which spread the two plough-chains was thrown down the bank.

This rope had a length of plough-chain fastened to the end and this culminated in a crook, which was hitched to a link on the front of the wheelbarrow. The rope was then thrown over the pulley, and the horse taken forward, with the Irishman keeping the barrow-legs clear of the ground. When the wheelbarrow appeared over the edge of the cut, it was unhitched, and the horse brought back to the post, by the time the second load was pulled to the top, the first man was down the bank and loaded.

Their leisure time was short, and all too scarce; but their requirements were simple - everything they needed came in skirts and bottles! To see them move from one canal to a new cut, was like watching the lines of refugees that we see today. There were columns of men pushing wheelbarrows and these were full of their tools - spades, shovels, mattocks and crow-bars. There were scores of horses in all stages of old age and infirmity, these pulled ramshackle carts of every description loaded down with cooking pots, fire-irons, heaps of the pitiful rags they termed bedclothes, harness used to pull barrows up the cut-bank, various goods belonging to the camp followers - who had no means of transport other than themselves, and amongst the heaps of rags would be placed the younger children, some of whom had probably been born on the canal edge.

What the horses could not pull was carried by the house-keepers and the other women in baskets. The camp followers were an essential part of the navvies' camp; but sadly they are remembered more for their nick names than their surnames, Squirrel-tooth Annie and Hoppity Jane, to name but two of them.

Cumberland was not a county which leant itself to canals - it probably had less canals per square mile than any other county in

Pictured left, Annie Cunningham (standing) the author's Irish grandmother and her mother, Frances.

England; but there was quite a bit of cutting done in the Carlisle-Solway area. After a preliminary survey a canal was cut from the Caldew at the Holme Head to join the river again past the Irish Gate bridge. This canal was not intended to carry shipping of any sort; but to provide power, and water for other purposes such as the factories producing goods of very description; which were built along its route. Nevertheless, although the canal was not designed to carry shipping, it had to provide a constant, powerful, volume of water, so at the Holme Head a dam was built where the river had cut deep through the centuries, and ran between high banks. When the dam was completed, the water level rose to the level of the canal, sluice gates could be closed if there was a violent flood, ensuring that any surplus water went down the Caldew. The building of the dam was a tremendous achievement then, when the only power was horse-power and the strength of a human arm!

As well as providing employment for others the contract was given to men who also employed Irish immigrants. They were as cheap as their cattle. Although the dam was not a long one by the standards of the day, it provided a great deal of work from the Irishmen, after the cutting was finished, the canal was to line for its full length with wet clay to ensure that no water was lost down the cracks in the rock strata. The clay was all to cart from pits sometimes two or three miles away.

The area we know today as Caldew Gate, was then known as "Little Ireland" - the Irish navvies made it their home; but it was not allowed to develop into the chaos of the usual navvies' camp. Housing of a sort was provided, even though you and I would probably have regarded the houses as garden sheds! The Irishmen were likely to be there for some time, as the Carlisle-Port Carlisle canal was still to construct.

For some strange reason the Caldew canal became known throughout its length as "The Dam", and there was the "English Damside" and the "Irish Damside". As Caldew Gate developed and streets of houses were built the term "Little Ireland" was gradually transferred to the inns - the "Irish Gate Tavern" and "The Blazing Barrel" where the Irish navvies, drovers and horse-dealers used to gather. In my boyhood (which is distant now) I can plainly remember ten factories, breweries and saw-yards, which were heavily dependent on "The Dam".

My great-grandfather Robert Blair was an Irish cattle-drover until arthritis began to affect his long distance travelling and seeing a block of old property for sale on the English Damside, he bought it, and operated a grocers and carriers business from the premises. There was living accommodation, apart from the shop and storage areas, stalls, piggeries and other outbuildings to the rear. He was not a canal cutter, but he came, liked what he saw, and stayed. Messrs. Oram bought the property when it finally came under the hammer and it was their first foothold in the city until they moved to more illustrious premises in Lowther Street.

The Canal Cutters, Carlisle to Port Carlisle

The Carlisle to Port Carlisle canal was a much bigger project than the "Dam" being roughly twenty miles long. The canal itself had to be wide enough and deep enough for two heavily laden barges to pass; but the most important constructions were the two Canal Basins at either end of the canal. These had to be extensive enough to act as loading and unloading bays for the many barges involved. The original excavations were on a mammoth scale, an eye witness said: "It was like looking at a human ant hill!" (This was the Carlisle Canal Basin).

The quarry sides were all to shape and build of stone and timer (all to cart from other areas). The method of excavation was still the same - the navigators, the wheelbarrows and the old, lame horses. Many more were brought in, some form other parts of the country; but a large number of them from Ireland.

The Solway end of the canal was to the navvies what the coal miners dreamed of "hitting a good seam", six feet thick, and a hundred-weight of coal falling at every pick-stroke. "A heavy sand" is the answer which most farmers between Brough and Silloth would give you if you were to ask what kind of land they farmed on. This is what the navvies found when they came to cut the canal. Beneath the sand was broken sandstone, which was easily handled. This was not good news for the contractors, however, for it was more porous, and required a thicker seal of clay.

The canal basin at the end of the canal which became Port Carlisle, had to be considerably deeper than the city one, to allow a small ship of shallow draught to enter, and leave on the high tide, lock-gates ensured the level of water in the canal remained constant.

At last all was finished and the canal could be filled. The opening ceremony was planned, and the luncheon which followed, was attended by the civic dignitaries, the factory owners, the financiers and their guests, plus the contractors. Of the real heroes of the piece - the navvies and the old, lame horses, there was no sign.

The navigators had moved on, some to new venues, some had gone home to the Emerald Isle, but some of the Irish stayed, and helped to swell the numbers on the Irish Damside, the beginnings of what we know today as Caldew Gate. In my boyhood the O'Tooles, O'Shawnessys, the Donnellys, Murphys, Donogues, the Blairs and the Cunninghams could have been found in Caldewgate, other parts of the city, and the area surrounding it. These were the descendants of men and women who had come to Cumberland for the canal-cutting, the railway building, and a host of other purposes, and stayed.

No doubt some of the lads who led the worn-out wrecks, which pulled the Irishmen's wheelbarrows, often dreamed of handling a better calibre of horse, here on the canal tow-path was their answer! When the canal traffic began, the number of horses required was considerable, also men, and lads to take charge of them - they might even be driving a team, if one barge loaded to the gunwales with factory products, was hitched in tandem behind another barge similarly loaded.

Even the weather provided work for the horsemen. For the duration of the Carlisle to Port Carlisle canal, the winters were some of the most severe that anyone could remember. In the depths of winter, the ice-breaker had to be kept going from 10pm to day break to ensure open water for the first barges through next day.

The canal water, unlike river water which is constantly on the move, was still and froze both quickly and deeply. The ice-breaker was built like a clod-crusher with a prow. The stern (rear end) spanned the width of the canal, and tapered to the bows, which were reinforced as they took the brunt of the ice-breaking. The whole thing was drawn by two horses, one on each side of the canal. This kept the prow in the centre where the ice was thickest. When the two lads reached the end of the run at Port Carlisle, they were provided with a hot meal by one of the Port horse-keepers and, after the ice-breaker had been turned around with a boat hook, the lads set off back with a fresh team of horses, arriving at Carlisle canal basin just as the first barge was ready to leave.

The Coming of the Railways

For a while the Irish men working on the canal thought that they had got to Heaven. The horses they worked with were a long way removed from the wrecks of time which pulled the navvies' wheelbarrows. Their work, though hard, was not the slavery they had been used to; their bread was sure for a number of years. The future seemed reasonably secure but, by the time some of the lads became middle-aged men, their way of life had changed forever.

Steam was in the ascendancy and, although it was confined to pumping water from the mines and stationary donkey-engines at the outset, eventually some enterprising soul, (there are some in every age), discovered a method of making an engine which propelled itself and, after some adaptation would pull a small train of coal tubs. Railways, of course, were nothing new. It was a common sight to see teams of horses pulling lines of coal tubs along wooden railways to the docks and other venues. The wooden rails were in the process of being changed to iron ones, when the steam engine came on the scene. The wood used was oak and, to its durability, there is ample evidence. A complete set of oak rails was excavated when a pit heap was removed recently in County Durham. The railway was equipped with a set of wooden points to change direction when required, and the whole set could have been used today, the state of preservation was so good.

Eventually attention moved from the mines to catering for the general public and the age of the steam railway was born. However the construction giants were not motivated by any sense of philanthropy. It was a case of: "get it, get it honestly if you can; but get it!" Once again the Irishman was the means of them achieving that state.

Undoubtedly other nationalities were involved but "Paddy" was in the forefront. This was the era of the Irish Potato Famine and, both in the years which preceded the "Famine", and those years which immediately followed, the unemployment rate in Ireland was exceptionally high; but during the years of the Potato Famine, the country was full of desperate men, and desperate men can be cheaply hired.

Those who contracted for the building of the railways knew this, and went to Ireland for cheap labour. They did their business with the "gangers", each ganger reckoned to speak for about fifty men, a position they had achieved by their size, their fists and their voice. They got the best terms they could for their compatriots, but even that was only a little better than slavery.

Those ship loads of Irish families who headed for the rail-roads, iron-works and factories, of the New World were guaranteed a job, but not high wages. The guarantee of a job had been achieved by the activities of the "Molly Maguires" an organisation which had turned murder into a fine art. Those who occupied the seats of power in this Irish Mafia enjoyed rich pickings from their fellow countrymen. Their rule was by fear and violence. Any iron-master, factory owner or rail-road builder who did not employ a large enough quota of Irish men in their work force, was liable to be found dead in a gutter, with a knife sticking between his ribs. Likewise, any immigrant from the "Emerald Isle" who was invited to join the "Molly Maguires" and refused, was thereafter a marked man. The organisation of course, ran the gauntlet of the "Pinkerton Men", who were the detectives who preceded the American FBI. But nobody "grassed" on the "Molly Maguires". The larger trade unions gradually took over their cause until there was no longer any need for their activities.

Happily the secret society did not exist this side of the Atlantic Ocean. Those who accepted the contract terms were guaranteed a free passage to England, though a lot of them would have been more comfortable if they'd swam across. The stench of their "free passage", hung around them for a week. They were transported to the port nearest to their assignment, as human ballast in vessels which can only be described as "coffin ships". These ships could be equated with the Black Hole of Calcutta, the notorious prison of Suraj-ud-Dowla. The Irish men were met when they disembarked by a representative of the contractors who had arranged for the men to have a meal, even though it was just tea, bread and jam. Men weakened by hunger could not fulfil the contractors' requirements, and many of them had fifty miles and more to walk to the site of their work.

The navvies' camps were no different to those of the Canal cutters. They built with what was at hand, and that was not much! The early stage of their work was not unlike the canal-cutting. The line of the track had been cut and graded level, or as level as possible, before the track was laid and, where the land became hilly and undulating, deep cuttings had to be made and here the brunt of the work fell on the navigators and their wheelbarrows, and the old horses.

Steam shovels and steam-driven "donkey-engines" had entered the scene, but the early types were not very manoeuvrable and the bulk of excavation and the disposal of the spoil, still fell to the lot of the navvies. The "donkey-engines" were stationary anyway. The saw millers on the line of the track were on to a bonanza as they supplied the sleepers to which the rails were fixed.

For a while the saw mill owners took on extra staff to cope with the demand. The work of the wood cutter was hard, but unlike the lot of the navvies, it was pleasant. Oak was specified at first but, as oak trees grew scarce, other wood was acceptable, provided it had been "tanked" (steeped in creosote).

After the first mile of track was laid, the materials for each succeeding "length" were brought forward by the "Puffing Billies", as the navvies called the early engines, and were unloaded at the end of the track to be manhandled into position by the navvies. The construction gangs worked separately from the graders and spoil-shifters; each group was responsible for a separate job. The sleeper men were in front of the others of course, laying the sleepers and packing the gap between with gravel. After a few cases of blood poisoning and septicemia, contracted from splinters off the wooden sleepers, the sleeper men were issued, after protest, with leather hedging mittens, which would deflect even thorns.

The sleeper men were followed by the rail-layers who carried the iron lengths, five men to a side, with long wooden handled pincers and laid the rails ready for the "pin-drivers". These were the strongest men on the pay roll and were responsible for driving home with sledge-hammers the iron pins which fastened the rails to the sleepers. Some could drive a pin home with one stroke but most needed two or three.

One of the railway contractors key men was assigned to each gang and he was responsible for the straight laying of the rails as well as the fastening of the "ties" between each rail and the one in front. The last part of his job was to rivet the threads on the end of each bolt, so that no nut would unscrew. As the men came to the end of their length, one of the "Puffing Billies" was right behind them, with another load of sleepers, rails, ties, pins, nuts and bolts, and gravel to bed in the sleepers. Here again the wheelbarrows were pressed into service.

When the surveyors reached the Shap Fells they had to solve a few financial equations, as well as geological problems, which confronted them. To tunnel was out of the question; to maintain a reasonably level pull would mean a tunnel twice the normal length, and the many air vents needed would take more constructing than the tunnel.

The quickest, and least complicated route was straight ahead, north over Shap Summit. The gradient could be reduced to where two engines could go over the top, pulling a train of coaches or wagons. This would be achieved by making the cuttings deeper than usual - more work for the navigators? Ah, yes - but they were cheap!

As they worked on the Shap to Penrith line they came within viewing distance of the drovers route known as "The Galloway Gate", along which herds of cattle, sometimes numbering a thousand made their way south in the direction of London. The route was also used by the trains of pack horses which transported the manufactured goods of the time as well as the minerals from the many mining operations, dotted about the Pennines.

As the drovers halted their herds for the mid-day break, they left them to fill their bellies, grazing on bent and mountain grasses which grew in profusion (in June) on the fell bottoms. Two of their number, mountain men, made sure that the cattle did not spread too far. The rest settled themselves on a grassy knowe, and attacked their frugal lunch, while their hobbled horses grazed nearby. The main topic of conversation would be the "Paddys", whom they saw in the distance scurrying backwards and forwards like ants, (60 per cent of the work force was Irish). When the wind was in the west, they could hear the ring of the sledge hammers - steel on steel.

Joe Fawcett's consignment of fell ponies - one of the last to be sold at the Ireby Horse Fair, circa 1930.

The navvies afforded the drovers quite a bit of interest, and sometimes amusement; they had no apprehension whatever about the factory goods, minerals and coal - apart from passengers - how wrong they were! In a matter of twenty years, their way of life had changed forever.

"From a field in the North to the block at Smithfield in 48 hours!" was the proud boast of the railway companies. Progress? I doubt whether the cattle, packed like sardines into the box-cars, together with the lethal horns with which most of them were equipped, would agree with you. At least, when they were part of a drove, they could spread about and get clear of a truculent neighbour.

The navvies, unaware that they were shaping the future for anything or anyone, drove their lines relentlessly north. The main lines were just a fraction of the work involved. There were thousands of acres of sidings, goods depots, shunting yards and engine sheds. When I was a school boy, my mother's parents lived quite close to

Boustead's grassing, a shunting yard which was part of the Carlisle complex. The over-head lights blazed all night and the chug-chug of the little shunting engines as they put together long trains of wagons loaded with various commodities for the larger engines to haul away next morning, only fell silent during meal breaks. The clash of buffer on buffer went on all night. The noise kept you awake for the first night or so then, I suppose that familiarity bred contempt!

The greatest achievement by the navigators, and the one which took the highest toll in lives, owning to the savageness of the terrain, the winters and the many cholera outbreaks, was the Settle to Carlisle railway. The grave yards of the parishes they passed through often contained more railway builders than the graves of local people.

Those of us who live in central-heated and double-glazed houses, with fitted carpets and every modern convenience, can have no conception of the human endurance involved in the building of the railway. If you caught pneumonia, and it was easy to do so at that altitude and in those conditions, there were no antibiotics then - it was a killer! A few, but not many, survived.

We can have no conception of the hardships they endured, apart from the work which was arduous. The navvies lived in shacks, which were little better than caves - indeed some did live in caves hacked out of the side banks, which abounded on he moor. The floors of each dwelling were carpeted with rushes, cut from the trackbed, and these were changed weekly. The clothes the navvies wore were often wet through and, if there was a severe frost through the night, they often had to batter their clothes with the back of an axe before they could pull them on. Of course, if the frost was prolonged, they slept in their clothes.

The crowning achievement of the whole project was driving a tunnel under Bleamoor, not long as tunnels go but, in the centre of the tunnel it was 400 feet below the surface of the moor. There were only three ventilation shafts; but what shafts! Here a new method was used - the spoil from the tunnel floor was extracted through the ventilation shafts and spread on the surface of the moor. The shafts themselves are more like vertical tunnels. They had to wide enough and strongly built to accommodate the tackle required to excavate the tunnel. Whether they used the eight horse wheel or the steam driven "donkey-engine" as a form of lifting power, I have never been able to ascertain. Certainly, whichever method was used, a considerable number of horses would be needed. The method used for transportation was a timber wagon drawn by twelve horses and, looking at the terrain on Bleamoor, I do not think it would be an exaggeration to say that a team of sixteen horses would be needed to move the "donkey-engine" to the site required. The Puffing Billies transported them to the end of the made-up track, then transported them to the timber wagons by man's ingenuity and the strength of horse teams.

When the lifting gear was erected they pulled the broken rock and clay from the tunnel-floor to the surface of Bleamoor. One thing is certain, there would be an army of Irish men with their wheelbarrows to load and unload the spoil, which was spread on the surface of Bleamoor.

Eventually the track for the last branch line was cut and laid and the last engine-sheds and sidings were constructed. The railways were completed, but there was a demand for a good man with a spade for the next 50 years. This was from an entirely different aspect of what we term "The Age of Progress".

Before we study this next phase, we must admit that the railways sounded the death-knell of the canals; they took the trade and made most of them redundant. Some, like the Manchester Ship Canal could adapt, and function still. The others went to the wall - the work and agony of a generation before were forgotten. There was no leisure industry then to save them, indeed leisure was as scarce as money. The Carlisle to Port Carlisle canal made up for the drop in the goods trade by starting a run for passengers. This did well for a few years until the shareholders began to claim for bigger profits, and the end came quickly. The canal was drained, the ports were dismantled, and after some alterations and time to dry out, the canal bed was levelled and a rail track was laid full length. This functioned as a horse-drawn railway till, round the time of the Great War. However: "It's an ill wind that blows nobody any good!" A large contingent of Irish men, and others, was needed for the conversion.

The Pipe-Track Cutters

About the time of the completion of the railways, the water companies were beginning to be formed. Piped water from being a novelty had suddenly mushroomed into a necessity and a profitable one at that! It was not difficult to interest the landowners in these schemes, for they could charge higher rents for farms which could boast of piped water to every house and field. Round the beginning of the 20th century and indeed till half-way through it, there were still farms which relied on every drop of water on the well in the middle of the yard, with the odd pond here and there for the livestock. The latter were notorious for spreading "Johnes Disease" and it is significant that, as piped water advanced, Johnes Disease became a thing of the past.

Some farms near a river were supplied to the farm house by a ram. This was simple and self-powered, but it caused a lot of headaches. The least interference with the flow caused a stoppage, it only needed a small fish or a frog to impede the current, and the ram ceased to pump until the offending creature was removed, then again round a bend in the river lying in the shallows was probably a dead sheep, seething with maggots, and it would stay there until the next flood removed the carcass. The rams did not deliver pure water, but served in a small way to provide the supply. As an acquaintance of mine once said: "You never realise how much water a cow can drink, until you have every drop to carry to it."

Before any pipe-tracks were cut, of course the reservoirs were to create, some man-made, some like Haweswater were lakes, and only needed a dam constructed across one end to raise the level of the lake, and thus increase the volume of water available. The man-made reservoirs were dams constructed across one end to raise the level of the lake, and thus increase the volume of the water available. The man-made reservoirs were dams constructed across dry valleys, through which a fast-flowing river ran, fed by tributaries, which in turn were fed by runners, which had their origins in he springs which rose amongst the cloud berries and the bog cotton of the moor.

Imagine a pipe-track stretching from Haweswater to the city of Manchester, with laterals off to other towns. The track for the main pipe had to be somewhat deeper and wider than the tracks cut for the supply pipes to each house and factory in the towns and cities which they reached.

There were no mechanical excavators in those days, or pipe-laying machines; just gangs of navvies, predominantly Irish, who cut every foot of those seemingly never-ending miles. They worked in gangs of ten men, and one was designated pace-setter. He was given four shillings more than the others per week, to ensure that the others kept up a good speed and, as they finished their lengths, they moved to the front of the other gangs.

The cottagers who supplied board and lodgings for the gangs were on a gravy train while the men were in their area. They themselves slept on shake-down beds on the living room floor; while the navvies occupied their beds, two or three as available. The Irish navvies did not occupy the beds, two to a bed; the usual ratio was two at the top and two at the bottom. The fact that the cottages were mostly "good meat shops", would probably make up in some small way for their uneasy sleeping arrangement.

Villages then were vastly different to those of today which are usually dormitories for commuters travelling between them and the nearest town or city. Villages then, except for a very few commodities, were self-sufficient, and to say that the pipe-track cutters boarded with cottagers is perhaps to convey a wrong picture of the scene. Cottagers were really small-holders; every cottage possessed half an acre of orchard which contained many varieties of fruit trees, besides holding some of their flock of poultry. Besides this a two acre meadow provided wintering for one or two cows and young stock. The village green was then a good deal larger than present ones, and was common grazing for the villagers' cows.

"Johnny Milburn the rabbit catcher," a character I knew in my early youth, gave me a clear picture of the scene as it was then. He would be in his late seventies when I knew him so his memories were of the mid-19th century. In his active days he used to farm a small-holding in the Croglin area and catch rabbits four to five days a week. When he was working a long way from home and had to board on the farm, his wife and family ran the holding. If they got into a tight corner the neighbours would help them out, for Johnny was a well-liked and reliable man. Should one of the farmers or their men fall ill, the cry was: "Send for Johnny Milburn" - he never refused.

Melmerby, he said, was typical of the villages of the time. On one of his rabbit-catching forays Johnny had to drive through the fellside village in the old milk float, which held all his rabbit-catching gear, ferrets and guns, and was drawn by a strong type of fell pony. He said the green at Melmerby would be roughly thirteen acres and was used by the villages as common grazing. Nowadays they have to pay somebody to keep the grass down!

There were, he said about fifteen cows on the green, and more cows and young stock down the side roads, which were used as pastures by the villagers. One of the old men was positioned about half a mile down the side roads to make sure the cattle did not stray too far. The two acre meadow which went with each cottage was grazed once the winter hay was secure. The women and children were called in at harvest-time to sheaf and bind and then the larger farmers allowed them the gleanings. The women used extra large hand rakes to row up what was left and borrowed horses and carts to lead the rakings to a big pike in each cottage's stack yard. This was threshed as required by flail and the resulting grain was fed to fowls and pigs. The pig stys joining each cottage were always full and the village pond was crowded most days by the ducks and geese belonging to the cottagers. This was the scenario behind the good meat shops; which offered board and lodgings to the navvies!

The pipe-track cutters functioned until 1945 when the mechanical diggers displaced them.

The "Tattie-Howkers"

West Cumberland by nature of its light land usually escaped the worst frosts and became a major producer of early potatoes - this was before Israel, Cyprus and Egypt had cornered the market through the supermarkets. The coal mines and the iron works were at the peak of their production and the pit-men, and those who worked in the steel-works, were the big spenders of the time. The early potato market was aimed at their purses and was a very lucrative trade. Ships sailed out of Whitehaven and other West Cumberland ports with their holds full of the early potato crop and unloaded them at the ports nearest to some of the big Midlands towns, where they were snapped up by people who were sick to death of peeling the wizened sprouted remains of winter. The Channel Island supply did not come further than the Midlands then, and West Cumberland could sell all the early potatoes it could grow.

The "tattie-howkers" were similar to the Scots fisher-lasses who moved down he fishing ports on the east coast of England for the herring gutting. They were similar in that their work was seasonal but, having done my share of both ploughing up and gathering the "tatties" - I would say that the Irish colleens had the heartier task. They formed themselves into gangs of twelve with one of their number acting as negotiator of terms for the rest. They did not work their passages as such, like the men on the cattle boats, the drovers were also dealers in flocks of Irish geese and they had standing orders for 2-300 birds for each of the larger farms, to clean up the waste potatoes, and then to graze the corn-stubbles after the gleaners had taken their shares.

As the drovers learned the venues of each gang of girls, (most of them went back each year to the same farms), they stipulated that, providing each gang would accept the responsibility of delivering a flock of geese to their farm, the drovers would pay their passage (it would not amount to much). This system usually worked out quite well.

When the ship disembarked its "cargo" at Whitehaven or whichev-

Joe Fawcett and Captain de Courcy Parry of Overwater Hall.

er port they used, the lasses set off, each gang driving a large flock of geese to their venue, which would be one of the bigger farms in the area. The honking of the geese would be heard half a mile ahead, and advertise the fact that: "The Irish were coming!" The geese were prepared for their road walk by being "shod". This entailed running the flocks through a long "foot bath" containing warm tar followed by one equally as long filled with sand. The tar solidified quickly, encasing the feet of the geese in a hard shell of sand.

The preparation for the "tattie-howkers" was begun a fortnight before their arrival. Two of the farm men's wives were hired for the duration of the "tattie-howking". The lasses always bargained for a cash wage plus board and lodging. The men's wives cooked and catered for the colleens. Each large farm possessed a "bothy" which consisted of a large room on the ground floor with a loft above and sleeping arrangements for the girls. The ground floor room had a large fireplace and an oven for cooking and baking.

The "bothy" was used by the Irishmen who came across for the turnip-hoeing, and from November onwards for the turnip-pulling, so it was never out of use for very long. The balance-ploughs (wheelers) used for digging up the potatoes, varied from one area to another, as each blacksmith had his own design, guided to a large extent by the requirements of his customers. The ploughs were a little lighter than the usual stitching-plough; which was used by the small farmers for both planting and lifting, but the bigger farmers who specialised in early and main-crop potatoes, kept the ploughs solely for lifting the potato crop. The potato ploughs were different to the stitching-ploughs in that they had no mould-boards. In their place was a grid of iron rods on each side, which let the soil through, and pushed the potatoes into two rows, one on each side. These were the forebears of the horse-drawn potato-diggers, and the colleens heaved a sigh of relief, when they say the potato ploughs which saved the lassies a lot of "sorting". The ordinary stitching-ploughs left everything mixed up together.

"Stitch" is a Cumberland term, from the Lake District south-wards the descriptive term is "drill". The riggs we see in old pasture fields are usually twelve stitch riggs; this was the breadth of a scythe-stroke - the old scythe blade was half as long again as the present ones, which are really designed just for cutting thistles. The sold scythe-men used to serrate their blades with a special chisel which made the blade cut easier and you could hear them make a rasping sound as the cut through the corn-stalks.

The "uniform" of a "tattie-howker" was a "coarse-brat". These were made with feed-bags and hemmed round with tape. Two tapes went round the back and were knotted in the front. About a foot of tape made a loop at the top, which went over the wearer's head. The aprons served a dual purpose - they kept the wearer clean and took the worst of the wear and tear. The girls worked in pairs and were given a "swill" (a basket of woven willow), which held roughly half a hundred weight and had a hand hole at either end. When the girls considered that the swill was heavy enough, they emptied it into the horse and cart which moved up the field along with them. When the cart was full, it was tipped at a long heap near the field gate. In front of all, of course, went the two horses pulling the potato plough, which was balanced depth-wise by the man or lad walking between "stilts" (plough-handles).

If the bridle at the end of the plough-beam - which could be moved upwards, downwards or sideways by the removal of a steel pin - were set right, it could be kept level by the slightest pressure on the plough handles. The cheerful chatter of twelve girls and the raucous cries of the rooks and sea-gulls which followed the disturbed soil are long gone, but today's potato lifting machine is no substitute for that scene. It made fifteen people redundant and there are no geese or pigs to clean up the discarded potatoes - in fact expensive sprays are needed to kill the rogue sprouters in the succeeding crop.

The colleens were ambidextrous and, if there was bull in the "tattie-howking" they could speed up the work in the harvest field. Half the girls made bands by knotting together two lengths of corn and the other half of the gang tied up and stooked the corn-sheaves. This released some of the farm men to catch up on other jobs. It is not generally known that, until the advent of the self-binder in the early 1900s, every sheaf was hand-tied, even the push-off reaper, invented around 1850, only made the sheaf, it did not tie it.

The self-binder was drawn by three Clydesdales, and it certainly took a lot of the drudgery out of the lassies' work. I knew personally the man who drove the first self-binder and its team of three horses in the corn-fields of Cumberland. Eddie Lorrimer was his name and he lived in East Nelson Street, Carlisle, towards the end of my school days. Eddie worked as a carter for Foster Bros. and originated in West Cumberland. He was tempted into Carlisle by the higher wages and better conditions offered by the firm. Arthur Forster was in charge of the horses and the outfits they pulled. He was a proud horseman, he kept the best and required good men to take charge of them. Eddie Lorrimer's wife was an Irish woman and it is quite probable that, before their marriage, she was a tattie-howker.

As the colleens had contributed to a successful "harvest home", by their band-making and sheaf-tying, they were usually invited to the "Kern supper", as the harvest home feast was called. The last ten cart loads of corn, which would normally have been stacked on he threshing loft to await the start of the winter feeding cycle, was built into a small stack in the stack-yard until after the harvest feast. The thresh-

Joe Fawcett from Lothian Gill and his wife, pictured while they were on honeymoon.

ing-loft was the perch for three to five fiddlers who provided the music for the harvest dance but, before this, of course, there was the feast. On every farm over 200 acres, there was a house with two boilers, or set-pots, each large enough to have held the laundry for a workhouse. Each boiler had a separate fire with flues which spiralled round the boiler. Both flues culminated in a tall chimney which ensured a strong draught.

On the day of the feast, the boiler which usually served the farm house on wash day, was pressed into service to boil in muslin bags five suet dumplings, each enough to satisfy six hungry people. The other one, which was used to boil the chat potatoes and the tail corn for the livestock, was fired in the early morning and, when the water was boiling two men carried a ham from the farmhouse kitchen, and plunged it into the "set-pot". When they deemed it was tender enough they raked the fire out and allowed the ham to cool in its own juices. Pigs were fattened to a greater weight then, and what are termed baconers today would probably have been classed as porkers then. Some used to buy a gilt carrying its first litter and, when the young pigs were reared, the gilt was fattened for the farmhouse, hence the large hams, which needed two men carried to carry them. When they judged the ham to be cool enough, two men carried it to the farmhouse to be cut into "collops" (slices) for the feast. About an hour and a half before the meal, the fire was re-kindled beneath the water used to boil the ham and, when this was starting to boil, a hundred weight of potatoes were emptied into the ham water and, as these cooked, they absorbed the flavour of the ham. Health and Safety Officers would probably have been struck down with apoplexy if they had seen such methods, but happily for the feasters, they were not around then. The water could be drained off the potatoes by the brass tap at the base of the boiler and was used the following morning to mix the pig-mash, whilst the mountain of potato peelings also found their way to the piggeries - nothing was wasted! Most larger farmhouses kept two maids with duties including hand milking, calf feeding and butter making; these two and probably two of the colleens, would have been baking a variety of fruit pies and two or three kinds of scones for three days before the feast.

Farmhouses were usually built with a front and a back kitchen, each with an oven, and this usually stood near the back door. A large quantity of bread could be baked in the oven at one lighting. The Harvest Home Feast was a great occasion, the highlight of the year. The corn was all stacked and safe and, once the main crop "tatties" were gathered, the winter could be faced. The Irish lasses had speeded the job up tremendously and were toasted in no uncertain manner.

A cask of ale would be brought by horse and cart from the local tavern; enough and to spare for all concerned. This was broached just before the feast and the various farmers whose Harvest Home it was were toasted for their generosity. A small cask of cider was the prerogative of the "tattie howkers". Another three weeks of good weather would see the end of the potato harvest and the lasses would be off back to Ireland - except for the small number who stayed if maybe, that the young man who followed the plough had decided that Mary O'Neil was the woman of his choice and this decision was mutual or that Maggie Rafferty had captured the heart of one of the carters. Quite often it was the farmer's wife who had taken a liking to Annie Malone and, knowing that one of their maids was leaving shortly to be married, she asked Annie to stay. For whatever reason they stayed - for the coming winter their bread was sure!

The "Tattie Howkers" Bath Night

Some of us bath once a week, some of us bath twice a day; but the "tattie howkers" had not the luxury of a hot water system to provide endless supplies of hot water. Imagine how many kettles of hot water (all to boil on an open fire), it would take to make baths for twelve young women, but the Irish lassies over came this seeming difficulty, as they did everything else.

Two of their numbers were detailed to do the laundry for the whole gang, once a week, and they joined forces with the farmhouse maids, who always washed on a Monday, as did most people then. The two large set-pots in the farm wash house, each of which was large enough to boil the laundry for a workhouse, were filled to the brim with water and the fires lighted beneath both boilers. When the washing was over, usually around 1pm, the boilers were topped up instead of emptied and the fires stoked up again to bring them to the boil. After an hour the fires were raked out and the water was left till around 6pm when the set-pots were hot enough to bath in but not to scald anyone. Two "coarse brats" (bran sacks made into towels by being hemmed round - sacks manufactured from jute), were placed to step out on to and a pile of "coarse brats" was laid ready to dry them off.

When the last colleen was inside, the door was bolted and windows curtained with bran sacks lest some of the local youths might be sent "over the edge" by the sight of twelve nubile bathers. Their illumination was by the light of two stable lanterns. Their method of bathing was four at a time two to each set-pot, legs and feet in the water, while they sat on the edge, and lathered from head to foot, before rinsing by submerging. Not for them the luxury of a bubble bath, their cleansing agent was a bar of Hudsons Soap - that was the "tattie howkers" bath night!

The Flail Men

These were the small farmers' travelling threshers, in the era before the mobile steam-thresher came on the scene. When the "tattie howkers" left for home at the end of October, a fortnight later saw the advent of the flail men who worked their rounds until the end of March, getting back to their starting point around the beginning of each month.

These men did not work their passage, like the itinerant farm workers, (I will describe their method of payment in a later chapter). It is possible that they paid their passage on the return trip at the end of the season, when they were "flush" with their earnings. The captains would know the men as they would use the same shipping line each year and were quite happy to put their passages "on the slate" - they knew the men would honour their word.

The large farmers made use of these men until barn threshers were invented when they adapted their barns to the new machines with power provided by the building of a four horse gin-case outside the barn wall. A huge cog wheel, the circumference of the building, was positioned at eave-height and vertical poles came down from this, to which the horses were yoked, and travelled round one in front of the other in a wooden alley way. A spindle (iron) came down from the centre of the cog wheel, and it connected by means of smaller cog wheels to a horizontal spindle which ran in a covered channel until it entered the barn wall. Once inside the barn, the power could be transmitted via belts, and pulleys to the machinery required - thresher, grinder, circular saw.

Those who were lucky enough to farm near a river used the water via a mill-race, and a water wheel to power their machines. Some constructed huge ponds, which held enough water to power a threshing and the water could be regulated by sluice gate. The ponds constructed were at some distance from the farm and, by skillful cutting of the mill race, the water had achieved a good speed by the time it turned the wheel. These ponds of course, by the end of the day, had fallen below the level of the mill race and it was a case of waiting a

The harvest field showing a two horse reaper known as a "push-off reaper" - photograph by Frank Meadow Sutcliffe by kind permission of the Sutcliffe Gallery, Whitby, for more information see www.sutcliffe-gallery.co.uk

matter of days, even weeks, before there was a good enough head of water to drive the thresher. The flail men were not governed by limitations such as this, and the smaller farmers were glad of their services. They went around in gangs of six and they could thresh two round stacks, roughly thirty cart loads, per day.

Three men flailed, two shook and stack the straw, while one forked sheaves to the flailers. Two of the farm staff loaded a cart in the stack yard and tipped a cart load in the barn door entrance, as the flail men required it. These men were fed by the farmer who employed them, and presumably, they fed well for flailing is a job which needs tremendous energy - half starved men soon tire. Flailing was a fine art and each man's flail was his own personal possession. It was no good giving a tall man a short man's flail or vice versa. A great deal depended on the way the beater was secured to the hand pole, strips of leather were threaded through the ends of each length of wood, then they were knotted together leaving the correct distance between the lengths of wood. A strip of leather wound round the others completed the job and the flail was ready for work. It looked simple when viewed from a distance, but unless everything was done correctly, the beater on the downward swing could strike the flailer a blow on the back of the head, that was capable of stunning him.

The smaller farmers, of course had no bothy to accommodate the gang, but what the flail men used to do was requisition an empty bothy within walking radius of the farms which required their services and pay for this with a day's work when they moved on.

The mobile steam threshers gradually usurped the role of the flail men, they could thresh, as much in a day as the latter could in a week. The flails were hung on the walls for the woodworms to destroy - what an ignominious end for such a useful tool!

The "Paddy-Lowpers"

These were the Irish men who cut the open drains in the hill country of Cumberland; they took their name from the giant spades used by the sod cutters in each gang. They usually worked in threes - one to cut the top sod, one to cut the next two spade depths and one to pull back the spoil with a draining hack. These latter were different from the muck hacks used when putting out heaps of muck from a cart; they had a more pronounced bend in the prongs than the others and the long pole handles were equipped with a spade box handle at the end which gave the dagger more power against the dead weight of the drain spoil, thrown out by the diggers.

The Paddy-Lowper (pronounced Lowper) were three times the size of an ordinary spade and had a flange welded onto the right foot rest to stop the users foot from slipping off and being damaged by the sharp edge of the spade. The shape of the Paddy-Lowper was this:

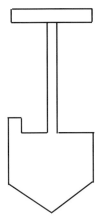

This is just a rough diagram, but it gives you an idea of what they were like - they were certainly more stream-lined than this and it was easy to see how they achieved their title; when viewed from a distance it appeared that the sod cutter "lowped" (jumped) on to the foot rest to send it down through the roots and the soil. The term was well known. You only had to walk into the nearest hardware store to the hill country and ask for a Paddy-Lowper, where upon the ironmonger would unerringly bring out the required tool from the back store room.

Cutting drains on "white fell" or heather moor was vastly different to working in the soft lands of the low country, which was regularly ploughed and loose to handle. This was the reason for the sod cutter using the Paddy Lowper. White fell was usually the home of flying bent, a variety of bent grass which grew exceptionally tall, and its habit was to grow from crowns which were six to nine inches apart as opposed to ordinary grass which covers the whole area. The roots seemed to grow deeper and tougher each year. I omitted to state at the outset that one of the tools required by the drainers was a scythe as the drainers worked on the moors from 1 April to 31 October. During the summer months the Paddy Lowpers had to scythe the length of the drain in order to get a straight cut. In October the seed stems and the grass blades became detached from the crowns and used to blow before the autumn gales, in some cases forming drifts and it was a common sight to see balls of dead grass driven before the wind, like the American tumbleweed. It is for this reason that the plant derived its name "flying bent".

The drainers were housed in the nearest empty shepherd's out-bye cottage, or a disused mine building which could be adapted to their needs. Their provisions were carted or pack-horsed out three times a week. Once would have been enough for ordinary men, but they never seemed to be able to make anything last. As one old acquaintance of mine once said: "You could take them a whole roasted sheep on the Monday morning, and they would have eaten it by Tuesday night - hence the twice weekly deliveries!

As the arrival of the Paddy Lowpers coincided with the busiest time of the shepherd's year, lambing time, they were often asked to cut the peats at the various mosses on the moor. Normally the peats had to wait until May, when lambing time was over, but three weeks extra drying improved the peat's quality - they hardened to the consistency of coal.

The work was similar to drain cutting; the top sod had to be removed to expose the good black peat and, while one man worked with the Paddy Lowper the other two hauled the sods to the edge of the peat hag and threw them into the bottom. The Paddy Lowpers were never allowed to get blunt - the sod cutter carried a file in a holster at the back of his belt and, when a large enough area had been cleared, the peat cutting began in earnest. One man cut the peats, one stood in the bottom of the hag and pitched the cut peats up over the edge where the third man loaded them on to a peat barrow and wheeled them away to the drying area on the heather. The hags were about three peats deep (4.5 feet) and the bottom one was the best burner. If there were two shepherds, as well as the farmer, the Irishmen would work on three mosses (three week's work); but they did not mind, they were well paid and, after all, they were fed whatever they did.

The Irish were credited with Herculean strength. There was even a giant hay-sweep drawn by two horses known as a "Paddy-Tippler". This was used to sweep hay together in the rows to build into large pikes to cure. After a week or so they could be led home and forked into the lofts and barns. If it was elected to stack in the field, the Paddy Tippler came into its own. It could drag a large pike (three quarters of a cart load) to the stack at a time and when it reached the required site, a lift on the handles (no mean feat!)would cause the sweep teeth to dig into the ground and when the horses were sent forward the Paddy Tippler turned a somersault on its swivels, and came down the other side of the hay pike, ready to set off again. The chains at each end, by which the horses pulled, were extra long so that when the Paddy tippler came over the top of the hay pike, the horses were well out of the way.

The drainers now could concentrate on their main tasks - after all that was why they had sailed across the Irish Sea, to cut open drains in Cumberland. The drains themselves were cut every seven yards and one chain to ten chains long, depending on the size of the wet area to be drained. Each drain was a Paddy Lowper and two ordinary spades deep (3.5 feet), the sides tapered from eighteen inches across the top to nine inches across the bottom. A chain measured 25 yards and was a form of measurement used by drainer and farmer alike.

Chain-making used to be a thriving industry in the Midlands until the tractor took the place of the horse. As well as measuring chains these manufacturers turned out chains of every sort - plough chains complete with swivels, chains for cart and wagon shafts, pike bogie chains, windlass chains for mine shafts and wells, anchor chains and many different types of chains for the timber world and a host of other purposes - it would need another chapter to describe them all. As there was no strain involved the measuring chains had a smaller link and were made of a lighter metal than the others. When the job was complete the farmer measured up with his chain and paid the men according to the price per chain agreed on at the start.

Well, the Paddy Lowpers have gone, the out-bye cottages and old mine buildings which they more or less camped out in, have tumbled down; but the drains they cut still run water - some of them over a hundred years old. The Kielder Forest covers thousands of them!

The Irish Gypsies

Those who think that the Irish gipsy and the horse dealer are one and the same thing could not be further from the truth. For one thing, the gypsies spoke their own language which was different to that of the horse dealers, even though both came from the same country. The Irish horse whisperers who were found in many parts of Ireland were found in either fraternity. That these men possessed an affinity with the equine race is beyond question. I have seen a long tail (unbroken two-year-old heavy horse) plunging, rearing and defeating the efforts of six men to get it into a blacksmith's shop, and the blacksmith had just given up in disgust and decided to throw the animal down and truss it up like a bullock to shoe it, when one of the Irish horse dealers came on the scene. He took hold of the halter shank, chatted the horse up with what we would term Irish nonsense, then turned on his heel and, leading the horse, he walked straight into the smithy and tied the horse to a ring in the opposite wall. He stayed until the blacksmith was finished and the horse gave no trouble.

One difference between the gypsies and the horse dealers was the fact that the former used to farm their horse, breeding a large number of their own semi-heavy types, even though they were often on the move. They bought and sold amongst themselves and, as regards the breeding side of their enterprise, they would buy a colt foal uncastrated, whose sire had probably been one of the commoner types of Shire, certainly not a pure bred one. This colt foal was brought on till it was rising two-years-old, then it ran with the breeding mares for two season ensuring a succession of foals. When it was castrated another colt foal had been brought on to take its place. Every colour under the sun was represented amongst the gypsies' horses - greys, blacks, browns and strawberry-roan, but the colour which predominated was black and white. No matter how much like the Shire they became barrel-bodied and hairy-legged - the black and white colouring of the original Irish pony seemed to dominate the rest of the colours!

Another way in which the gypsies differed from the horse dealers,

Typical gypsy horses pictured being washed in the River Eden at Appleby New Fair, photograph by Peter Koronka.

was the fact that the gypsies only went back to the Emerald Isle every two or three years, probably for some special gathering of the particular clan to which they belong, or for some important horse fair they wished to attend. The horse dealers crossed and re-crossed the Irish Sea four to five times a year in the course of their trade.

The point of their entry for the Irish gypsies was usually Whitehaven, it being the nearest landfall to Ireland, but as this fraternity kept no records, either financially or historically, we have to rely on experience and word of mouth and, after seventy odd years I can lay claim to both. No true gipsy would give you a bad deal. If we were ever "taken for a ride" it was by what we would term "roadsters". The gypsies were free spirits, they had a code of honour and lived by it as the following narrative will testify.

A farm at Kirmington near Grimsly relied heavily on two gypsy families to thin their swedes, turnips and mangolds. They had taken the contract for three years previously and had done a good job.

During the fourth season the mother of one of the families collapsed and, although her condition was not life threatening, she needed a greater degree of care than could be provided in a "Varda" or living-van. The farmer's wife did not hesitate; she took the woman into the house until she was fit to cope and sent a hot meal down to the Varda every night.

One local girl came in daily to see to the needs of a large poultry yard and the cream and butter from three cows. One girl was resident and she helped with the cooking and the housework, so the gypsy woman's illness did not over stretch anyone.

When the time came to settle up the two families gave a full day's thinning to pay for the woman's keep. In the meantime the garth man, who worked amongst the cattle in the stock yards all winter and helped with the summer work after turning out time, happened to mention to the gypsies that they had just lost the stock yard horse which was a great favourite and would be hard to replace. About a week after the gypsies had gone the farmer noticed a black and white Shire type horse amongst the work horses which ran in a field adjoining the stack yard. On asking the garth man if he knew anything about it, he was told that one of the gypsies had brought it saying that there was nothing to pay. Its name was Dan and it would do anything - it carted hay, swedes and bedding into the stock yards for the next ten years.

About the same time one of the farm men noticed a strange mark on one of the trees near the entrance to the farm land. It was cut so deep that it could not be eradicated. On making enquiries, the farmer discovered that he had been given the highest accolade the gypsy fraternity could bestow. Now every gypsy family which passed that way respected the farmer as "the man who helped the gypsies."

When the Vardas disembarked on the West Cumberland coast it was late May. The turnip-hoeing was not far away and grass was growing by the foot. They immediately turned their horses in the direction of Rosley Great Fair which they would reach as darkness fell. The twenty acres allotted to the gypsies was illuminated by the many cooking fires round which the families sat. Late-comers would pass lines of horses staked out on the road side verges, getting longer as each Varda was unyoked. They not only had the horses which pulled the Vardas but also strings of mares, foals and horses for sale as well as traps, flat carts and sets of harness. The forty acres on the opposite side of the road was used for the cattle fair and divided into four enclosures to accommodate the various types, while a half-acre paddock was kept to sort the various lots in. In the centre of it all was the hub of activity - the parish tavern and, although the sign read "The Rose and Crown" I never heard it referred to as anything other than "The Camp", taking its name from the gypsies encampment. Most business was concluded in "The Camp" and, as the ale went down, the yields went up. "She'll milk like a tap!" was the usual claim - the buyer would probably need a tap to make up the difference in milk yields. The feats accomplished by men and horses were phenomenal. At one Rosley Fair a buyer from a distance was heard to remark to the landlord: "These men must be tremendous workers!"

"Yes," said the landlord drily, "It's a great pity that they do it all here!"

However, it was not all disappointment. A friend's father bought a smart pony, a tub trap and a set of harness from the gypsies for £60. It was 1913 and it was in daily use for the next 30 years, (with a change of pony of course). Then the trap was pushed into the back of a hay barn where it stood for 50 years. Two years ago my friend thought that he would see whether the trap was worth anything, so he cleaned it up and offered it for sale at Wigton Spring Horse Fair - it made £850!

After the fair was over and the Irish gypsies had spent a week with their own kind, they would take to the road again, the mares and the foals in he string behind the Vardas, together with any horses they had bought. Taking in Ireby Horse Fair, they would head for Appleby Fair which lasted a week and hosted, (they would have been told) gypsies of every nationality. Here some of their horses would be sold and undoubtedly they would buy some for breeding purposes and some to re-sell. You never saw a bankrupt gypsy. It was an unwritten law amongst the fraternity that if one fell upon hard times through horse disease or accidents beyond the control of man, the rest of the clan were in honour bound to make up the horse herd to its original

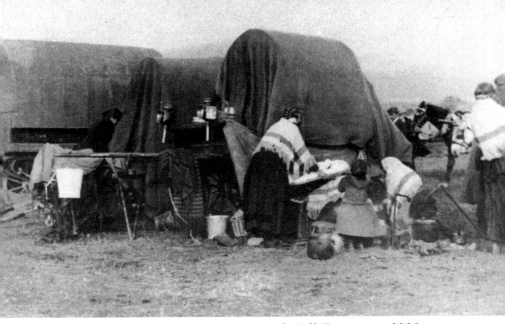

Travellers preparing dinner at Brough Hill Fair, circa 1900.

size. This code persisted even amongst the urbanised gypsies, those who had become householders and made a living carting for builders and joiners, and providing a cheap removal service for the locality. One such I remember from my school days. These men were known as "long cart men" by some and this man's horse had died suddenly. It was 1932 and a time of recession; he could not afford to buy another one. His uncle however, had done very well for himself and possessed seven horses and contracts for several years ahead. It was he who provided the horse which got his nephew on the road again after only two days.

There was one gypsy clan which used to winter in the Yetholm area and they elected their own King and Queen. After Appleby Fair was over, the gypsies would take to the road again, probably heading east for the Yorkshire Wolds and Lincolnshire where there was more free grass available. Only the horses which pulled the Vardas were shod. All the rest had their hooves dressed periodically by the owner or his family.

They would pass close to Brough Hill which was the venue for an autumn horse fair and to which they would return in October. The autumn fairs were just as important as the spring ones, and attracted quite a large section of the gypsy people. There were three large fairs in Lincolnshire to where they were headed - Brigg Fair, Horncastle and Louth. South Yorkshire also hosted a few horse fairs.

The free grass to which I alluded earlier was mostly found in Lincolnshire and South Yorkshire, the area which formed a strip of marshland beside the sea and extended from roughly mid-Yorkshire to the bottom end of Lincolnshire and was known as the "Carrs". Every village, householder and private farmer whose property bordered the Carrs had grazing rights on them. As the householders usually didn't exercise their privilege, the gypsies often had a horse herd grazing on the Carrs, as long as the herd did not reach alarming proportions, nobody came forward to complain. The worst thing that you can do to a horse is give it too lush a pasture; the Carrs being rough grazing and rushes combined, were ideal for horses.

Another venue the gypsies made great use of was the canal banks. There must have been hundreds of them dotted over the two counties; you did not go very far without crossing a canal. They were fenced off from the surrounding farm land, so the gypsies had ready made fields, albeit long ones. The gypsies occasionally used these during the summer but, between fairs, there was a good deal of farm work they could do and the road sides were wide enough to tether their horses on.

The canal banks were mainly used for wintering on and it was quite common to see two or three Vardas parked together on a wide part of the bank and a horse herd grazing on either bank. A friend of mine, who was a better mathematician than me, reckoned that the three families had 150 acres of free grass amongst them.

They always camped near a long stretch of willows, for here was the material which formed the basis of their winter industry - basket making. They liked yellow willows for butter and egg baskets and for clothes baskets for carrying the washing to and from the drying area. Green willows were preferred for garden trugs, turnip and potato swills. The gypsies were also good wood carvers and out of ash they could make wooden harness for horse work, also single-trees and double-trees for horse chain work, snare pegs and clothes pegs were other winter specialities. When they had a large enough variety manufactured they set off with horse and long cart to hawk their wares round the surrounding farms.

To see a group of gaily coloured Vardas parked side by side on the canal banks, with the cooking fires blazing merrily in front of them was a sight not easily forgotten. One linking van might have two black and white stallions rearing in mock battle either side of the door, another might have scrolls of flowers back, front and sides, while yet another had tiers of cornucopias either side of the door!

Occasionally the gypsy section of society threw up personalities who had a great influence on the rest of humanity. One such was Gypsy Smith, the great Methodist preacher at the turn of the century, who toured this country and the USA more than once. Also Rev. Bramwell Evans, who was himself a Methodist preacher and naturalist of note. The Central Hall, Fisher Street, Carlisle, was packed to the doors at each of his lectures on nature. He wrote many books on the subject under the pseudonym "Romany" and periodically took to the road in a gypsy Varda.

Well, it becomes harder and harder now to find a gypsy family living in a horse-drawn Varda. Logically, if the countryside continues to be swallowed up by the maw of the developers, and the motorways and the relentless march of mono-culture is not stopped, in a hundred years time the only grazing left will be the canal banks - and they will certainly not be free!

The Horse Dealers

From the time the carrion birds picked the bones clean of every horse carcass which littered the arid plains of Mesopotamia after those early battles, the horse has been pushed to the forefront to further the avaricious ambitions of a war-like section of humanity. Men had made use of the horse far earlier than this, but the earliest records we have of any clarity, mention a Syrian war camp surrounded by picket lines to which were tied horses, riding mules, baggage mules and asses, which were also used as pack animals.

The war chariots used by the Babylonians, Persians and the Roman armies were pulled by teams of four horses. The huge unwieldy siege-engines often needed twenty horses to move them. Once gun powder was discovered, six horse teams used to draw the gun carriages. Every war from the Napoleonic Wars until 1939, and for a few years after each one, was the crock of gold at the end of the rainbow for the Irish horse dealer. They probably functioned much earlier than this, but the time of which I write was the hey-day of it all.

The casualty lists of men engaged in each war were colossal, but thousands of horses and mules perished cruelly and for the wounded there was no hope. My father was an eye witness to the plight of the horses during the great war 1914-18. On the Western Front the Menin Road was one of the supply routes and mule teams hauled supply wagons constantly along its length and gun carriages with their six-horse teams risked the German gunners who had the Menin Road within their sights - it was just inside their range. Father said that all might be quiet for three days then suddenly all hell was let loose and after each barrage a man with a pistol was sent out to deal with the wounded horses. When a direct hit had been scored there was just a jumbled heap of equine carnage. Sometimes there might be two left alive out of a team of six, but the only sign of life was perhaps a twitching of a limb which made the clouds of carrion birds, which covered the carcasses, lift momentarily. Sometimes there would be one solitary horse standing and things looked more hopeful; but when

A ledge wagon built by Tom Tong of Bolton, photographed at Brough, circa 1911.

the man with he pistol drew lvel with the outfit he saw that, although the horse was still half-harnessed to its dead team mates, when he looked more closely there was probably a rear leg dangling, shot through by a bullet. For the horse there was only the final trumpet...

This went on on every front and after every battle. All these horses were to replace, their numbers had to be made up. The Crown agents for the Armament stables were everywhere - each horse fair saw one or two of them in attendance and they always went with the best. One of my friends told me that his neighbour was ploughing next to the road with a fine team - probably the best pair of horses in the parish. One of the Crown agents happened to be passing along the road in a pony and trap and got his eye on them. Pulling the pony up he sharply tethered it to a tree and strode across to where the farmer was ploughing. After a cursory look over the two horses he requisitioned them for the Army. The price he quoted was adequate but the horses had to be unyoked there and then. The agent fetched a couple of rope halters from the trap and the harness was left festooning the plough.

This was happening all over England and this was where the Irish horse dealer came into his own. He bought from the fairs of Donaghal to the port of Dublin, or the lairages of Belfast, from which two ports he could either head to Silloth and West Cumberland or Portpatrick and Stranraer en-route for Northumberland and Durham. Their destinations depended to a large extent on the breed and type of which their particular string of horses was composed.

They had many different outlets for their horse and many ways of dealing with them from May onwards. When they got back from a trip to England, they would buy up all the worn out horses en-route as cheaply as possible - cab-horses, coach-horses, every corporation stable would be a Mecca for them. The horse buses and dust carts needed young, active, animals and the streets were notorious for affecting the feet of horses through time and rendering them unfit for heavy work.

When they were buying young active animals to re-sell in England, their strings seldom exceeded 25; but aged and infirm horses gave little trouble so they were not averse to extending their numbers to 36 en-route to the fattening grounds. They all worked in a different area and all had their following of farmers who would take a couple of horses at a time for six weeks fattening. Their money was sure - they were paid after each consignment.

After six weeks the horse dealers would probably send two of their agents to collect the whole string and take passage on the cattle boat which plied between Dublin and Portmadoc in North Wales, then head for the meat markets in Liverpool and Manchester. In the 18th and 19th centuries there were butchers who specialised in horse meat in every large city. The dealers would make a good profit from the fattened horse, their agents would only have their own riding ponies left and these would carry them back to the ship and home.

Ireland, having a large population of the bigger type of donkey, was in a good position to breed quality mules. The very small farmers and small holders did all their work with large donkeys. Carts were made to donkey size and ploughs and reapers were manufactured so that they could be pulled by two large donkeys. When the dealers were offered worn out cab horses and the throw outs from the horse bus stables, they ran a critical eye over them and picked out the best mares. Although these were unfit for hard work they would breed foals for two or three years and the dealers re-sold these to the mule breeders - the rest went to fatten. The mule breeders were larger farmers who incorporated this activity with the rest of their farming, crossing the mares with a large donkey stallion and selling the mules at three-years-old to the dealers as broken to chain work. Many of the horse dealers had contracts with the Army to supply a certain quota annually of mules for pack work in mountainous country and to pull baggage wagons. the dealers could ask a high price and their bread was sure. It was a common sight, a century ago, to meet a string of mules and their attendant Irish men heading for the nearest Army depot.

An acquaintance who had been one of the horse keepers in charge of an Army re-mount 1914-18 camp, set off along the picket lines to inspect a consignment of mules which had just been delivered. A fellow horse keeper accompanied him, keeping a respectful distance from their heels, as they were all of them notorious kickers until they'd been handled. My acquaintance's fellow horse keeper stopped abruptly behind a magnificent specimen of mule. It was a grey and must have been 17 hands high. The man's admiration must have over-ruled his caution because he stepped a little bit nearer and, just at that moment the mule lashed out with both hind feet and took the top of his skull off, like taking the lid off a tin. He did not die, but his war was over.

I had two direct links with the horse dealers during my school days in Brampton, North Cumbria; one was human and the other was an equine representative. One of my childhood heroes was Dick Megahy (pronounced Megee). Dick was the local horse dealer and could do anything with a horse. The strings of horses no longer

German gypsies pictured at Brough Hill Fair, circa 1900.

came; that they had in previous times a tavern in the centre of the market town bore witness to - it was known as "The Strings of Horses". Its inn sign depicted two men in 19th century attire and a line of horses stretching into the distance. The tavern had probably been the half-way stop for the Irish horse dealers on their way from the Solway Plain to the coal and lead mines of the North East.

Dick Megahy was the horse dealer I mentioned earlier who could lead a "long tail" (unbroken horse) into a blacksmith's shop when five men and the blacksmith couldn't force it in; he seemed to have an affinity with horses. Dick's father was an Irish horse dealer who was well known in Brampton area as a man with whom you could have a fair deal. He scoured the length and breadth of Ireland for the best and he had breeds and types for every season and a horse for every purpose under the sun. When Dick was a lad he brought up the rear of each string and his father rode in front. There was always a demand for the Irishman's horses - just try to imagine a world in which the petrol engine was unknown - that was the era in which Dick Megahy's father traded as a horse dealer. To give you some idea of the number of horses required, my old friend Bart Dunn, who died recently, was fourteen-years-old at the outbreak of the Great War and was sent to work on the Colliery farms at Ashington. He said that it was a common sight at hay time to pass 60 different horses and pike-bogies leading hay to one of the Colliery stack yards. Six stacks would be going up in every stack yard and they were long stacks, each one as high as a house when finished.

There were two horses at each stack yoked to a low-geared pulley and, as each hay pike was slid off, the grab spikes were lowered and kicked in; then the horses were sent forward and they could lift a pike in two grab loads. Bart reckoned that there were upwards of 200 horses above and below ground; when we realise that this was only one of at least 30 collieries in Northumberland and Durham, plus West Cumberland, and the rest of the country, we begin to understand what an important man the horse dealer, Irish or otherwise, was.

When Dick's father reached the end of his run, he bought worn-out horses on the way back. The woods were one source of these; a horse had to be fit and in its prime to work in the forest hauling timber; five years and most of them needed replacing. It was a hard life for man and beast in the woods. Dick's father had various farmers in the brampton and Bewcastle areas who fattened horses for Robert Megahy - he had his own outlets. When his father gave up horse dealing in 1920, Dick married a horse dealer's daughter and they made their home in Brampton. The strings of horses no longer came from Ireland, but Dick kept the fattening bases until 1950.

I mentioned earlier that I also had an equine link with the horse dealers - this was Old Sammy. Sammy was a nondescript Irish Clydesdale, one of three long tails bought by Joseph Jefferson of Townfoot Farm, Brampton in 1913. The three young horses were bought from Robert Megahy to break in and re-sell the following March; but Sammy, by his sunny nature and many likeable qualities had become everybody's favourite and was kept on. Townfoot Farm does not exist now. Then it was the largest farm in the area with 400 acres and also home of an illustrious Clydesdale stud; but none of the horses stays in the memory like Sammy. He could be used by women and certainly was during the Great War. He was still on the scene in my late school days and, despite the fat that he was semi-retired and approaching 30, he still did a bit of light winter carting for the shepherd. My last glimpse of Sammy was of him galloping along the side of a hedgerow amongst half a dozen yearlings - I hope that he gallops yet in those "Elysian Fields".

The Jack of all Trades

The couplet reads: "Jack of all trades, and master of none", but this could not be said of the Irish itinerant farm workmen - they were experts at many different tasks and the farmer was glad to see them come. Many of them "worked their passage" - this does not mean that they helped with the sailing of the ship; they came over on the cattle boats and their work was associated with he cattle. Before the ship sailed from Dublin via the Isle of Man to Silloth, they prepared the pens in he hold, erecting and bedding them ready for occupation. They helped to pen the cattle, making sure that the weight was evenly distributed, lest it interfere with the steering of the ship. There was nothing more that they could do until the end of the voyage when the ship berthed at Silloth where the cattle disembarked. After the ship berthed at Silloth, the Irishmen let a pen full of cattle up the ramp at a time, allowing the other men time to water each bunch at a trough, and stall them individually in the lairage. When the last of the cattle had gone up the ramp, the real "passage working" started.

The return cargo would be, more than likely, dead stock crates and sacks of cattle food and miller's offal etc., consequently the hold had to be left absolutely clean after the cattle had gone. The first thing the Irish men did was dismantle the pens and stack them clean ready for the next consignment of cattle. Next the muck was wheel barrowed to the front of the ramp and a grab was lowered from the quay side. It was then wound up and dumped in a waiting fleet of horse and carts provided by local farmers. when the muck became too thin for the grab they wheeled it up the ramp in the barrows. When the captain was quite satisfied, the Irish men set off for their eventual destinations. Those bound for West Cumberland kept to the coast road, those of whom I write set off across country. As the crow flies 25 miles to Lothian Gill in the Low Hesket area beside the old M6.

Joe Fawcett who died 30 years ago was an eye witness of these men. Joe was born in 1876 when his father was bailiff for the family who farmed Lothian Gill which was the largest farm on the west-

Joe Fawcett pictured with his eldest daughter, Grace.

ern slopes of the Sand Ridge, which ran roughly from the Carlisle gibbet at Harraby, to the Penrith gibbet at Thiefside. All the farms in the area were large ones and most relied heavily upon the Irish men for their summer labour force. Supplying Lothian Gill with food was like delivering to a hamlet. There were two large houses, one of which was the bailiff's and it alone would hold the bailiff's family and six single men plus two maids. There were six cottages containing horse ploughmen, carters and two cattle men and, of course, the Irish men's bothy which held six men from mid-June to mid-December. Joe said the butcher cart was in the yard every day (there were no fridges then of course).

It may seem a huge staff for a 400 acre farm; but not when we realise that the farm was merely the centre of a vast cattle and sheep dealing empire. Hundreds of acres of summer grazing were rented and, besides which, the family owned a large slaughter house in the city of Carlisle. Most of the single men who "lived in" at Lothian Gill, could be employed droving the cattle and sheep to and from the fairs, as and when required (petrol engines were still in the future). By the time of Joe's birth the early two horse mowing machines had been introduced making the scythe men redundant, but his father could remember them coming, year after year, their extra long blades dismantled and blade and shank wrapped tightly round with strong sacking to avoid damage to any other person, and the all important blade. The scythe men were there from the end of June until the end of September when they came to the end of the grass cutting and the corn cutting was ready to start. Joe's father said he had four good scythe men on the farm staff who joined the six Irish men to make a cutting gang of ten on the first day, which usually resulted in half a field cut the first day. There were very few fields on Lothian Gill that were less than twenty acres. After this they were on their own, they could be pressed into other jobs, but they were principally scythe men.

The Irish men we are interested in usually came after mid-June for the turnip hoeing and, staying on these six Irish men were both well fed and well paid; their affluence depended on the fact that they worked like slaves. The fist job they took on contract was the turnip hoeing. If the turnips were clean of weeds a reasonable rate per hundred yards was settled on but, if weeds proliferated, the price went up accordingly. The "King of the Dealers" always had a 30 acre field of turnips himself, plus a 20 acre field which belonged to one of his neighbours; but he did not negotiate for this field until the autumn, by which time he could judge what kind of crop the turnips would make. By the time the men had finished hoeing the 30 acres, the first field of clover hay would be ready to lead, and the Irish men were put to this. Some farmers used to pike the hay, and lead it home on the pike bogies, but this was not the method used by Lothian Gill.

When the hay was deemed to be ready, it was built into good sized hay cocks, then loaded on to horses and carts to lead home. If it was decided to stack a field to lead later, it was left in the rows, and swept to where the stacks were being built, using a pair of "paddy-tippers". If it was decided to lead the hay home, this is where the Irish men again came into their own. The carts were each enlarged by being fitted with shelvings and these were suitable for either loose hay or corn sheaves; if they were loaded by an expert - as the Irish men usually were - they looked like miniature long stacks on wheels.

The Irish men were paid a certain figure for each cart load and eight carts were employed, three in the field, three in the stack yard and two somewhere along the route to and from the field. The same method was applied to the corn leading, when the corn was ripe enough for cutting, the Irish men took the stooking at a set price per stook. The women and children from the cottages were paid to make corn bands and tie the sheaves dropped by the two "push off" reapers, the Irish men followed on - five sheaf rows to a stook.

There was no over-time then but, after the harvest feast every man or woman who was employed on the farm was given a guinea (the Irish men included). The latter worked hard, but they did not lack entertainment; apart from the fiddle music which they enjoyed, they were given the use of the shepherd's cob and the milk float to drive to the city (Carlisle) every Saturday night after 5pm where they could visit the taverns or the music halls, whichever their choice. The four fast transport horses kept at Lothian Gill were all our of Clydesdale mares, served by a hunter stallion ensuring that they were both strong and fleet. Two horse and rubber tyred digbies were at the disposal of the boss and his family, one outfit was attached to Joe's father and his family and the last last was at the disposal of the shepherd, and of course, the Irish men on Saturday nights. Joe said that every time they set off his father used to threaten them with the withdrawal of all privileges if there was a scratch on the outfit when they brought it back - Joe never heard of one.

October was the month in which every cattle shed was cleaned out in readiness for the winter's intake of fattening cattle; all the muck being carted out on the stubbles or hay meadows. In all roughly 150 acres received this treatment and the Irish men had it all to spread at a set price per heap. Joe said that it was like watching machines go down the field - you wouldn't believe that a human being with a muck fork could work so fast. From 1 November till they returned home in mid-February, two days a week were devoted to the barn thresher. This meant that the rest of the farm's staff carted sheaves into the barn and forked them onto the threshing loft to be put through the threshing machine by those in charge, the power being provided by four huge Clydesdales turning the cog wheel in the gin-case. Meanwhile the Irish men formed themselves into two gangs - three of them handled the straw while the other three dealt with the sacks of corn as they came off the thresher.

Most of their work from 1 November was turnip pulling which, of course, could be taken on piece work. Here the local small-holders entered the scene. Most of the large farms on the Sand Ridge let out their turnip sheep (fattening enterprise) to outside tender and the turnip sheep could be fitted in between the small holder's morning and weaning stock work. The usual payment round the turn of the 20th century was one shilling (5p) for every fat sheep which was sold off the farm. It may not sound much, but when you consider that a shilling bought as much as a £5 note does today, and a large farm like Lothian Gill, with their own field of turnips and the twenty acre field of turnips rented nearby, they would fatten 2,000 plus by the end of the winter, so a shilling a sheep totalled a fair sum. Turnips is a collective noun encompassing swedes, mangolds and Aberdeen yellows. The first job the Irish men did was to pull 100 cart loads of Aberdeen yellows, to be carted and pitted for lambing time. The Irish men covered the pits with wheat straw and soiled this up to a thickness of three inches, leaving a ventilation ridge along the top of the pit - turnips needed to breathe they were told.

At Lothian Gill a large number of cattle were fattened during the winter; bullocks in large sheds (loose) and heifers tied in the many byres. These were all catered for from turnip houses situated at strategic points in the vast complex of buildings.

When the Irish men had pulled a large enough acreage of swedes to allow the carters to fill the turnip houses, they could concentrate on the sheep breaks. All fattening sheep then had the swedes cut for them into slices twice the length of fish fingers and a Blackstone turnip cutter was the favourite. Six turns of the handle on a newly-toothed cutter and you had a swill full.

A weight could be bolted to the rim of the balance-wheel on the opposite side of the cutter. This increased the power and made the swinging of the handle less of a slavish task. The first break was the largest; it included the acreage which provided the 100 cart loads of Aberdeen yellows and the six rows (four drills to a row) which made a line of heaps (five cart loads to the heap), along the front of which were fastened the sheep hurdles, thus effectively fencing the break off from the rest of the turnip field.

The ratio of troughs required (corn and turnip) was one trough of each type to every ten sheep, so the carters would be fully occupied for a full day, carting out the equipment for the turnip sheep. The shepherd filled the bins with corn weekly (it was a mix of various ingredients) and when the small holder found the sheep increasingly dependent upon cut turnips, he brough a member of his family with him to fill the hopper with swedes while he himself carried out the cut turnips to the sheep. By the time the Irish men had pulled the second field of swedes into six-row breaks, it was the end of February and the end of their contract. They could collect their money and head for home on the next cattle boat.

In the 1940s Britain suffered some of the worst winters in memory, culminating in the winter of 1946-7 when the country was blanketed with snow from December to April. There were few snow clearing

Appleby New Fair - selling horses on The Sands. Photograph circa 1925.

machines and the War Agricultural Committee set up ten hostels in Cumbria to house Irish men who worked on the farms until it snowed and then were issued with shovels and put to snow clearance.

The Irish Drovers

Irish cattle have been on the scene from time immemorial; I could not even guess when the trade began. The Irish drovers were men of a superior calibre; they knew the country to which they sailed, even the individual requirements of each farmer, and types of cattle needed in the various areas of each county they travelled though. They carried this information in their minds on their buying forays to the West of Ireland.

The 1500s and 1600s were particularly risky centuries for the drovers. The cattle boats then had a very small displacement and carried considerably less cattle. The Irish Sea was a formidable barrier between England and Ireland and, if a storm blew up half-way across, it was a traumatic business. Sailors then had to climb rigging and do a balancing act on the main masts. No wonder they periodically needed press gangs to augment the crews; but the old adage still holds good: "One volunteer does the job better than ten pressed men!" Even with the sails furled, they could be driven by the storm on a rocky shore, miles away from the point of landing. The Irish Sea was the grave yard of hundreds of cattle and drovers - casualties of early ship wrecks which were probably never recorded. One advantage the sea voyage offered was the fact that there was no West, East or Middle March on the water. They could by-pass any Border warfare and put in at a port further down the coast. The Highland drovers would have to run the gauntlet of cattle thieves and robber barons - they had no choice.

In the early days of droving, the Irish men drove their cattle round from fair to fair until they had sold the last of the ship load. As time went on however, the reputation of Irish cattle's ability to fatten spread far and wide and the drovers often found that the supply was short of the demand. The early Irish cattle, like their drovers, were looked upon as a lesser breed and, when they turned up at a cattle fair on their itinerant journeys, they were given the worst area - the Irish end - they called it. This act of segregation rebounded in the Irish men's favour for, as the cattle's ability to thrive became more widely known, the graziers used to head for the Irish end first. The cattle used to fatten quickly and they were rather cheaper than the others.

Strangely enough, the cattle were not known by their breed or cross, but by the area from which they originated - the Doneghals. They were big, rangy, cattle; what their sire was I have never been able to ascertain, but that there was Shorthorn in their background somewhere was obvious. They had short curved-in horns and, in colouring they were mid-way between the South and North Devon, a yellow tinged with red. They looked what they were - weight makers.

The bull most often used as a crossing sire then was a big, rangy type of Aberdeen Angus. Although this particular cross was common all over Ireland, the crosses from a large area round Letterkenny seemed to do best. These were known as West of Ireland cattle and this cross on the dairy Shorthorn cow with the Aberdeen Angus bull was a smooth-skinned blue-grey heifer or bullock. There were some farmers who based their dairy herd on blue-grey cows - these inherited their milk yields from the dairy Shorthorns and their increased butter-fat from the Aberdeen Angus and, when the main production of the dairy was butter-making, this would be an important factor. The smaller Kerry and Dexter herds, mostly found in the southern counties of England, all originated in the crofting townships of southern Ireland, from where they were shipped along with other breeds and crossed from Cork to disembark at one of the south coast ports.

When the Argentinian craze for "baby beef" started, it nearly ruined the British Aberdeen Angus. Daylight under the belly weighs nothing on the scales! This was one of the excuses used by the herd owners as they bred their cattle with shorter legs; but what they forgot was that short legs inevitably carry short frames, with a resulting lighter weight. When the Argentinian craze, like the South Sea Bubble finally burst, the "baby beef" men found their cattle dropped like the proverbial hot coals. Fortunately the Irish men still had a large reserve of big rangy Aberdeen Angus bulls to draw on and so the British breeders were able to pull back from the brink.

Epilogue

O f all this vast concourse of Irish people and animals, there is now no trace except that the thoroughfare which runs eastwards from Whitehaven's' harbour is called Irish Street. Whitehaven as a sea port has fallen from great heights to its state of glorified marina. In former days the lasses who were the tattie howkers drove their large flocks of honking geese eastwards, the strings of horses were disembarked and all round them was the sound of ship building. The many dry docks were full of slave ships in various stages of construction. "Coffin ships" they were known as, for many of the slaves died on the journey from Africa and the West Indies to the southern states of America. There were ships loading at the coal staithes, and others unloading casks of run, brown sugar and treacle. In the background was the continual tread of horses hooves as they carted coal in and other commodities out. Now there is only a deep silence, nothing to signify that Whitehaven was one of the main ports for the Irish to the North of England.

I have enjoyed writing this record of the past; the characters came alive as I wrote. Indeed many of them, like Dick Megahy and Johnnie Milburn, the rabbit catcher, were still part of the scene during my boyhood and youth. The lowing of an approaching herd of cattle could still be heard, for the Irish men reckoned their legs were the cheapest form of transport. Nowadays they travel from A to B in cattle transporters. I am sorry for the writer of memories a hundred years from now, they will be very arid.

Some of the old American Indian chiefs of the 19th century were shrewd philosophers. One made this observation shortly before his death:

"Only when the last tree has been felled, only when the last river has been poisoned, the last fish caught, and the last acre has ceased to grow, only then will the white men realise that you cannot eat money!"

After 75 years of observing this phenomenon, I'm inclined to agree with him.